ADVENTURE CHALLENGE
GRANDPARENTS & HERO MENTORS

REACH OUT!
hello@thesociablebunny.com
LEARN MORE!
www.thesociablebunny.com

Copyright © Sonflower Press, LLC
All rights reserved.
No part of this book may be used
in any manner whatsoever
without the written permission.

Published 2019, Sonflower Press, LLC
ISBN 978-1-7338043-2-5

Dedicated to
YOU...
A loving parent, grandparent,
or hero mentor
who is embarking on an exciting
adventure
with the child of your heart.
Get ready to
watch the wonders unfold!

TABLE OF CONTENTS

Part 1 — **TRANSFORMATIONAL LEARNING**
SQJ Explained 1

Part 2 — **18-WEEK CHALLENGE**
Bunny on the Move 7

Part 3 — **BASE CAMP PREPARATION**
How it Works! 17

Part 4 — **TREK TO THE SUMMIT**
Personalized Journaling 33

Part 5 — **YEARLY MILESTONES**
Catch them Being Good! 145

What in the world is S.Q.J.?

It's **NOT** an airport in China...
It's **NOT** new...
Or the latest fad...
Or even a brilliant invention...
In fact, it is as old as history itself!

It's all about:

S. STORIES

Leading through:

Q. QUESTIONS

Into Personalized:

J. JOURNALING

S.Q.J. is just a name we gave this transformational method of learning. So what makes **S.Q.J.** so transformational?

1. **STORIES** create a memorable way of learning new ideas through someone else's experience.

2. **QUESTIONS** lead us to wrestle with new ideas and process what they really mean.

3. **JOURNALING** helps us personalize how those ideas could be lived out in our own daily lives.

S.Q.J. is the **"SECRET SAUCE"** that propels learning **FROM EDUCATIONAL TO TRANSFORMATIONAL!**

The projected outcome of applying S.Q.J. to

1. As children practice each new character quality within themselves, they grow in **maturity and confidence**

2. As children practice each new character quality within their family, they grow in their ability to develop **functional family relationships**.

3. As children practice each new character quality within their circles of influence, they build up their community and create a **positive atmosphere** wherever they go

So let's continue by introducing an additional tool to make it
EVEN MORE FUN!

For best results in building noble character with The Sociable Bunny Series, add
BUNNY ON THE MOVE!

This fun tool is used at home and gives parents/grandparents/hero mentors an easy way to:

1. Start stimulating conversations
2. Build a shared vocabulary
3. Track and celebrate progress

"THE SECRET SAUCE"
is found in
REINFORCING AT HOME,
what the child is
LEARNING IN SCHOOL...

All of this happens across 3 generations!
  GEN 1... The Grandparent
  GEN 2... The Parent
  GEN 3... The Child
  And it looks something like THIS:

S. STORIES

The **TEACHER** and students read **LET THE ADVENTURE BEGIN!** Read a chapter per week. Students may read ahead...most will want to!

Q. QUESTIONS

The **STUDENT** works through their *ADVENTURE ACTIVITY BOOK!* This 18-week adventure explores weekly character qualities...thereby establishing a common classroom vocabulary.

BUNNY ON THE MOVE!

The **PARENT** initiates the ***BUNNY ON THE MOVE!*** to introduce the new "word-of-the-week" and to connect the Child with their Grandparent/Hero Mentor. For best results, if the parent has time and energy, they can build excitement by hiding the bunny daily and discovering their own stories in the **ADVENTURE CHALLENGE JOURNAL**.

Skype or

J. JOURNALING
ADVENTURE CHALLENGE DATE

The **GRANDPARENT/HERO MENTOR** visits or video chats with the child weekly for an Adventure Challenge Date to play "Hot-and-Cold Hide-and-Seek"...thereby engaging in real time, even across vast miles of separation. The Grandparent asks key questions and shares stories from their own **ADVENTURE CHALLENGE JOURNAL!**

Video chat

Trek to the Summit
18-Week Challenge: Tracking Progress

At the end of each week, after your child completes their activities and hears stories from their parents and grandparents, have them glue the new character quality to the poster on their wall. The Grandparents could whoop and holler to applaud their progress! Your child is learning how to complete a huge project one little step at a time. Setbacks happen and sometimes we fall down. But we pick ourselves up and keep pressing forward...*TO THE SUMMIT!*

Summit Celebration...
3 Generations of Noble Character in Action!

It's time to celebrate! Invite the aunties and uncles! And, of course, the Grandparents! Share favorite stories you remembered from your life or heard from one another. And remember to praise and affirm anyone who might have demonstrated truly noble character in action! Don't be afraid to admit the times you failed. Noble Character takes a *LIFETIME* to develop!

To begin, turn page

BASE CAMP PREPARATION

Essentials for Success

Get Ready!

You are embarking on an exciting adventure of discovery! You will be joining your child on an 18-week challenge to build noble character and become a truly great friend.

Whether you are a Parent, Grandparent or Hero Mentor, "your Child" will refer to the child of your heart.

What an honor and privilege! You must be a very special person. Your child trusts you enough to invite you into their life.

You now have the power to influence your child for a lifetime.

You will be using your own stories and mature perspectives to prepare your child to handle LIFE!

**What will your child need from you?
1-2 hours a week!**

30-60 minutes in your journal to discover your stories and 30-60 minutes with your child on your Adventure Challenge Date to exchange stories and play BUNNY ON THE MOVE!

The next Three Big Ideas from your child's Adventure Activity Book will help you understand your role on the Adventure Challenge Team.

① 18-Week Adventure Challenge
TREK TO THE SUMMIT

HOW DO YOU CLIMB A HUGE MOUNTAIN?

...ONE STEP AT A TIME!

You may think some activities are too hard!
Guess what...You can do it!
One activity at a time.
If you keep going without giving up,
you will succeed and that's a great feeling!
Don't be afraid to ask for help when you need it.
It's even more fun together!

② Adventure Challenge Team!

If each member of the team does their "bit" the best they can, everybody wins! We reach the SUMMIT together.

Building Noble Character

CHILD
The Student Cooperates...
Using the magic word (OK!) while completing their activities.

GRANDPARENT
The Mentor Encourages...
Inspiring growth by sharing their own stories.

PARENT
The Parent Facilitates...
Hiding the bunny and connecting the Team.

Reaching the SUMMIT...
The team members become "truly great friends", **creating a positive atmosphere where ever they go!**

*Did you notice the rope tying the team together for safety and success?

3 Confronting Coyotes!

- You may run into coyotes on your adventure.

- Coyotes can be sneaky!

- Did you know we have coyotes hiding inside our hearts?

- Sometimes they howl ugly lies to scare us! "You're not good enough. Don't even try! You're too stupid. You're a failure!"

- And sometimes they drool and whisper sneaky things to kill our dreams.

- "You don't want to do that. It'll never work. It's a stupid sissy idea."

- And then there's the sneakiest coyote of all. He stops us in our tracks!

- You know what he says? He whispers in our "down-ear" in a voice that sounds like our own.

- Very quietly he says… "I don't want to…" And all progress stops!

- So how do we beat our coyotes?

- Stand up tall and say, "Be quiet, sneaky coyote! I have a goal to reach! I am going to make it to the Summit and enjoy a Celebration like you have never seen. Just watch me!"

Ideas for Bonding with your Child

① READING IT TOGETHER
Read *The Sociable Bunny,* LET THE ADVENTURE BEGIN!

② TRAVELING BACK IN TIME...
You will have the opportunity each week to explore your life memories. Who knows? You may gain surprising new insights into how amazing your life has been and how the challenges have helped you grow into the person you are today. Then you can share your stories as you connect with your child in deeply meaningful ways...helping them grow strong and become a truly great friend that others can trust, enjoy and respect.

3 PARENTING DO OVER

When thinking of how unique your child is and all you've learned over the years, what would you do differently in raising your child if you knew then what you know *now*? Try applying that with your child during your Adventure Challenge Dates!

4 SHARING PASSIONS

Encourage your child to tell you about things they love doing. Let them teach you! Then teach them about the things you love doing. They will feel unique and valued by you.

(Do you live far away from your child? If one of your passions is gardening, you could send them seeds and teach them how to care for a plant. If your child loves video games, they could teach you how to play with them, either by phone or on-line gaming!)

1

BONZO ON THE MOVE

(fold up)

2

FLUFFULL ON THE MOVE

(fold up)

Begin building a new family story today!

FREE DOWNLOAD AT
www.thesociablebunny.com

3
BUILDING NOBLE CHARACTER
Tracking Poster

1. Unique
2. Sting
3. Comfort
4. Friendship
5. Influence
6. Adventure
7. Empathy
8. Celebration
9. Courage
10. Full of Love
11. Giving
12. Positive
13. Perseverence
14. Fear
15. Honest
16. Cherish
17. Encourage
18. Leadership

4
18 CHARACTER QUALITIES

Preparing for Your Adventure Challenge Date

1. Have fun! First, foremost, and always!

2. Discover your unique stories for the week by answering journal questions

3. Parent cuts out the new Word-of-the-Week and places it on the bunny with kisses

4. Parent HIDES the bunny and tells Grandparent where it is hidden

5. If connecting with your Child from a distance, schedule with the Parent to set up your Adventure Challenge Date.

Your Adventure Challenge Date

1. Have fun! First, foremost, and always!

2. When you meet up for your Adventure Challenge Date, you could say:
    a. "I'd love to hear what you learned in your Activity Book this week about (character word). Especially in the part where Fluffy Wonders about Your World!" Then listen!
    b. When your child has finished sharing, ask "Would you like to hear a story about that from my life?" Then share what you wrote in your journal. You may also want to share what you answered about your Child to encourage them in their growth.
    c. Then play **BUNNY ON THE MOVE!** Hot-and-Cold Hide-and-Seek.
    d. When your child finds the bunny, ask excitedly "What's our new word for next week?"
    e. Then watch them glue the new word to their poster. "Wow, we're making progress!"

Congratulations!

You're ready to leave Base Camp...

Let's get started!

Let the Adventure Begin!

My child's name is _____.

I will complete my Adventure Challenge Journal every week on _____ (day of week).

I will meet up with my child every week on _____ (day) at _____ (time) by video chat or in person for an Adventure Challenge Date. (*Some weeks may require re-scheduling as life happens*).

Our 18-week Adventure is set to begin on _____ (date).

We are planning our Summit Celebration 18 Weeks later on _____ (date).

If possible, I will add Yearly Milestones of Noble Character and present this journal to my child upon completing elementary school in _____ (year).

Call Parent to hide BUNNY and schedule Adventure Challenge Date: _____ (day) at _____ (time)

_____ (signature) _____ (date)

Chat with your child..."Let's find **BUNNY ON THE MOVE!** and glue our first word to your poster to get started!"

Part 4

PERSONALIZED JOURNALING

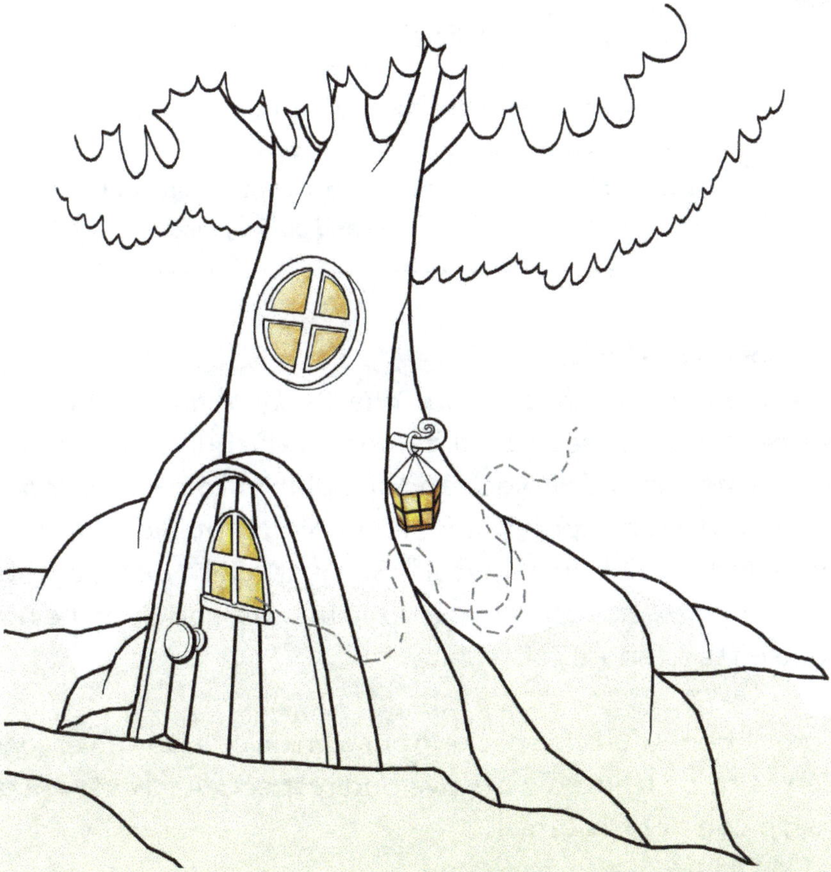

WEEK 1: UNIQUE
PEEKING INTO MY CHILD'S ACTIVITY BOOK...

FLUFFY

All the bunnies in Bubble Burrow had color!
Some had gray fur. Some had brown.
And some had lots of colors, all mixed up.
Fluffy thought they were beautiful!
They thought she was "different".
Her fur was as light as a snowy day.
Long arms made her hop in a very strange way.
Mama tried to make her feel better
and told her she was pretty in her own special way.
But Fluffy felt strange and out of place.

YOU ARE UNIQUE!

Being unique means that you are "one of a kind" and not like anyone else. Fluffy was seen as "different" by the bunnies in Bubble Burrow. She felt out of place and she didn't like that feeling. It made her feel scrumpety! Fluffy is learning that every bunny is unique and special, even herself! She just might discover that she has a lot to learn from her unique friends, and that she has unique gifts to share too!

We are all beautiful and special in our own unique way. Everyone deserves to be treated with love and respect. And every relationship can help us grow!

Sharing My Life Stories with My Child

How was I unique as a child? How did I feel about my differences?

How might those very traits have shaped me as an adult and contributed to those around me?

Looking back, what have I learned about being unique and embracing my differences?

"Parents with their words, attitudes, and actions possess the ability to bless or curse the identities of their children."
—CRAIG HILL

Putting Myself in My Child's Shoes...Being Unique

In what ways is my child unique?

_____
_____

How do I see my child handling their uniqueness?

_____
_____

How might I use my own story to encourage my child to embrace their uniqueness and use those very traits to help them grow in noble character?

_____
_____

Are there other stories I might share about a unique person or animal?

_____
_____

"Teach your child they're unique. That way, they won't feel pressured to be like everybody else."
—CINDY CASHMAN

What Could I Possibly Say to Encourage My Child?

I like you just the way you are! You're special to me!

You make a difference in people's lives. You're irreplaceable!

You are such a bright child! Never be afraid to be yourself.

What have you learned from your friends today?

Do you feel accepted by your friends for who you are?

Your worth is in who you are, not in what others expect you to be.

Not everyone will like you, and that's alright!
It happens to everyone. Don't force yourself to
"fit in" just so everyone will accept you.

Always remain true to who you are.

What I will choose to say when I see that my child is struggling with their uniqueness?

_____
_____
_____
_____

*HIDE THE BUNNY!
Or ask the Parent to tell you where it is hidden, and confirm Adventure Challenge Date with Parent!
(date) _____ (time) _____

"When teaching your kids about the concept of respect, teach them of their worth as a person."
—CLAIRE STRANBERG

Adventure Challenge Date
WEEK 1: UNIQUE

"I LOVE YOU, FIRST, FOREMOST AND FOREVER. NOW LET'S HAVE FUN!"

1. What did you discover in your Activity Book this week about being Unique?
2. Like Fluffy, you are unique and special and have gifts to share with others! In what ways do you see yourself as unique?
3. Do you ever feel like your friends are more special than you are? What do you admire about them that makes you feel that way?
4. Have you ever put stings into your own heart by comparing yourself with others? What can you admire in yourself?
5. Would you like to hear a story from my life about being unique? (Share from your journal)
6. Is there anything else you'd like to talk about?

BUNNY ON THE MOVE!

Let's find the bunny! *(Play Hot & Cold—Hide & Seek)*
What is our new word for next week? *Stings*
Let's glue it to your poster. Wow, we're making progress!

"Children will listen to you after they feel listened to."
-JANE NELSEN

Tracking My Trek
THE WEEK IN REVIEW

What cool things or concerns did I discover about myself this week?

_____
_____
_____

What cool things or concerns did I discover about my child this week?

_____
_____
_____

How did I use my life story to inspire my child?

_____
_____
_____

What new ideas might I try in the future because of my discoveries?

_____
_____
_____

WEEK 2: HANDLING STINGS

PEEKING INTO MY CHILD'S ACTIVITY BOOK...

BONZO

When it came time to hop home, Fluffy said,
"This was a fun adventure, Bonzo Bunny!
I like you. Will you be my friend?"
His eyes blinked fast
and he snapped at her in a boyish way.
"Yuck. That's mushy! I don't like ugly girls."
Then he turned his back and hopped away
as fast as he could go.
"Ugly?"
The word stung her like a bee..

STINGS

Stinging words inject poison into our hearts and cause painful wounds. They often focus on what a person looks like on the outside and not in their tender heart. Stings hurt! They make people feel rejected. Bonzo used a stinging word to push Fluffy away. Did you know that when one friend stings another, it is possible to mend the friendship? Five very powerful words are: "I'm sorry. Please forgive me."

Choosing to forgive is a powerful medicine that removes the poison from our hearts.

Sharing My Life Stories with My Child

How was I stung as a child? Or even as an adult? And how did I handle my stings?

How did I sting others? Why did I choose to be unkind? How did I mend my broken friendships?

Looking back as an adult, what have I learned and how might I have handled stings in a better way?

What story can I share to inspire my child?

"Don't worry that your child never listens to you; worry that they are always watching you."
—ROBERT FULGHUM

Putting Myself in My Child's Shoes...Stings

Does my child have a tender heart that's easily stung?
How does my child handle stings?

Does my child have a hard heart that stings others?
What might be motivating my child to act in unkind ways?

How might I use my story to encourage my child to handle stings in the most positive way?

Are there other stories I might share about handling stings?

> "At every step, the child should be allowed to meet the real experiences of life; the thorns should never be plucked from the roses."
> —ELLEN KEY

What Could I Possibly Say to Encourage My Child?

Are you hurting from something a friend did to you? The pain will go away once you forgive him...

Why do you think this person said that to you?

You are so courageous about forgiving and asking for forgiveness! It requires a lot of courage!

Have you said a stinging word lately that you'd like to take back?

Don't ever use a stinging word just because you've been stung.

I know you can handle it. I trust you!

Your choices matter, they will become your tomorrow!

What I will choose to say when I see that my child is struggling with stings?

_____

_____

_____

*HIDE THE BUNNY!
Or ask the Parent to tell you where it is hidden, and confirm Adventure Challenge Date with Parent!
(date) _____ (time) _____

"A child who is allowed to be disrespectful to his parents will not have true respect for anyone."
—BILLY GRAHAM

Adventure Challenge Date
WEEK 2: STINGS

"I LOVE YOU, FIRST, FOREMOST AND FOREVER. NOW LET'S HAVE FUN!"

1. What did you discover in your Activity Book this week about Stings?
2. How would you have reacted if you were in Fluffy or Bonzo's shoes?
3. Tell about a time when someone stung your heart with their words. What happened and how did it feel?
4. Tell about a time when you put a sting in someone's heart. How did that make you feel? Did you use the five powerful words? ("I'm sorry. Please forgive me...")
5. Would you like to hear a story about handling stings from my own life? (Share from your journal)
6. Is there anything else you'd like to talk about?

BUNNY ON THE MOVE!

Let's find the bunny! *(Play Hot & Cold—Hide & Seek)*
What is our new word for next week? *Comfort*
Let's glue it to your poster. Wow, we're making progress!

Tracking My Trek
THE WEEK IN REVIEW

What cool things or concerns did I discover about myself this week?

What cool things or concerns did I discover about my child this week?

How did I use my life story to encourage my child?

What new thing might I try in the future because of my discoveries?

WEEK 3: COMFORT
PEEKING INTO MY CHILD'S ACTIVITY BOOK...

MAMA

Mama looked so good
standing there in her apron.
Mama kissed her up-ear.

"You are not ugly, Fluffy.
Little boy bunnies just say things like that
to little girl bunnies at your age.
And maybe Bonzo has a sting
in his own heart
that makes him say ugly words."

COMFORT

Comfort means easing the pain of someone who has been hurt!
Fluffy knew Mama was kind and wise, so she hopped onto her lap and cried. Mama listened quietly. Then she used kind words to comfort Fluffy's hurting heart, speaking truth to heal the sting of Bonzo's lie. Mama also helped Fluffy care about the stings in Bonzo's heart.

We have the power to comfort others with kind and loving words. When we are hurt, it's great to find a wise loving friend to help us process the event. It also helps when we seek to understand what might be motivating others to be unkind.

Sharing My Life Stories with My Child

How have I grown in giving and receiving comfort?

How was I comforted as a child? What comforts me as an adult?

How have I given comfort to others?

Looking back, what have I learned about giving and receiving comfort?

What story can I share to inspire my child?

"Children are our second chance to have a great parent-child relationship."
—LAURA SCHLESSINGER

Putting Myself in My Child's Shoes...Comfort

How can I encourage my child to find comfort and to comfort others?

How do I see my child seeking comfort?

How do I see my child giving comfort to others?

How might I use my own story to encourage my child to give and receive comfort in the most positive ways?

Are there other stories I might share?

"It is easier to build strong children than to repair broken men."
—FREDERICK DOUGLASS

What Could I Possibly Say to Encourage My Child?

*I hear you, sweetie. You're safe with me!
I'm right here for you! I'm not going anywhere!
Everything will be all right, you'll see!*

*I'm so sorry you have to go through this,
I know how hard it is!
Is there anything I can do to help you feel better?*

*Let's come up with a solution together...
No matter what, I'll always be on your team!
You're enough and I appreciate you so much!*

What I will choose to say when I see that my child needs to be comforted?

_____
_____
_____
_____

*HIDE THE BUNNY!
Or ask the Parent to tell you where it is hidden, and confirm Adventure Challenge Date with Parent!
(date) _____ (time) _____

"Each day of our lives we make deposits in the memory banks of our child."
—CHARLES R. SWINDOLL

Adventure Challenge Date
WEEK 3: COMFORT

"I LOVE YOU, FIRST, FOREMOST AND FOREVER. NOW LET'S HAVE FUN!"

1. What did you learn in your Activity Book this week about Comfort!
2. When feeling hurt like Fluffy did, do you share it with someone who can comfort you, or do you keep it to yourself? Why?
3. Has anyone ever comforted you? Who? What did they do or say?
4. Have you ever comforted anyone? Who was it and what did you say?
5. Would you like to hear a story about comfort from my own life? (Share from your journal)
6. Is there anything else you'd like to talk about?

BUNNY ON THE MOVE!

Let's find the bunny! *(Play Hot & Cold—Hide & Seek)*
What is our new word for next week? *Friendship*
Let's glue it to your poster. Wow, we're making progress!

Tracking My Trek
THE WEEK IN REVIEW

What cool things or concerns did I discover about myself this week?

What cool things or concerns did I discover about my child this week?

How did I use my life story to encourage my child?

What new thing might I try in the future because of my discoveries?

WEEK 4: FRIENDSHIP
PEEKING INTO MY CHILD'S ACTIVITY BOOK...

BRINDLE

On her first day at
Bubble Burrow School,
Fluffy met Brindle,
so shy and sweet.
They liked each other
the moment they met.
Fluffy's heart sang,
I have found a friend at last!

FRIENDSHIP

Friendship is a special bond the grows between those who like and trust each other. In a classroom, everyone is unique! Some are friendly and others are shy. You may think the shy ones are not friendly, when they might just be afraid to reach out. Kai-Pono wants you to know that every bunny wants to be loved and accepted. On Fluffy's first day of school, she showed courage by saying "hello" to Brindle! Her reward was a great new friend! We can enjoy wonderful friendships when we reach out to others.

A true friend is one of life's greatest gifts. Sharing with a true friend doubles our joys and diminishes our sorrows.

Sharing My Life Stories with My Child

How have I grown in building strong friendships?

Who was my closest friend as a child and what did I enjoy about that person?

Did that friend help me grow and cause me to stumble?

Looking back, what have I learned about the importance of friendship?

What story can I share to inspire my child?

"Love is giving your kids your undivided attention and time."
—KEVIN HEATH

Putting Myself in My Child's Shoes...Friendships

How can I encourage my child to build strong friendships?

_____

_____

Who is my child's best friend? Do I know what they like about them?

_____

_____

How do I see that person helping my child grow into their best-self?

_____

_____

How might I use my story to help my child choose the most positive friends?

_____

_____

Are there other stories I might share?

_____

_____

"The kids who need the most love will ask for it in the most unloving ways."
—RUSSEL BARKLEY

What Could I Possibly Say to Encourage My Child?

*Spending time with you is one of my favorite things to do!
I will always want your best and help you in every way I can!
You can always count on me!*

*Who are your favorite friends? Why?
Do you feel you can trust your friends?
Is there anyone who is hard to be friends with? Why?
How do you feel about making new friends?
What kind of friend do you believe you are?
Do you feel comfortable with your friends?
I love being friends with you?*

What I will choose to say to build a strong friendship with my child? Or when I see my child struggling with friendships?

_____
_____
_____
_____

*HIDE THE BUNNY!
Or ask the Parent to tell you where it is hidden, and confirm Adventure Challenge Date with Parent!
(date) _____ (time) _____

"Encourage and support your kids because children are apt to live up to what you believe of them."
—LADY B. JOHNSON

Adventure Challenge Date
WEEK 4: FRIENDSHIP

"I LOVE YOU, FIRST, FOREMOST AND FOREVER. NOW LET'S HAVE FUN!"

1. What did you learn in your Adventure Activity Book this week about Friendship?
2. Feeling comfortable with someone means you feel safe enough to be yourself, and that you trust your friend to still like you. Who are the people in your life who help you feel that way?
3. Have you ever had a good friend like Brindle who likes you just the way you are? Who is it and what do you like about them?
4. Have you ever been that kind of a friend to someone? Who is it?
5. Would you like to hear a story about friendship from my own life? (Share from your journal)

BUNNY ON THE MOVE!

Let's find the bunny! *(Play Hot & Cold—Hide & Seek)*
What is our new word for next week? *Bullying*
Let's glue it to your poster. Wow, we're making progress!

Tracking My Trek
THE WEEK IN REVIEW

What cool things or concerns did I discover about myself this week?

What cool things or concerns did I discover about my child this week?

How did I use my life story to encourage my child?

What new thing might I try in the future because of my discoveries?

WEEK 5: INFLUENCE & BULLYING

PEEKING INTO MY CHILD'S ACTIVITY BOOK...

BELLA

It felt like she'd been punched in the heart!
Like a dozen bees were stinging all at once
as every bunny in the class
laughed at her
and turned away.
Fluffy hardly heard a word
Teacher said that morning.
She was too busy tugging on her down ear
and feeling the stings in her heart.

INFLUENCE

Influence means causing someone to change how they think or act, for better or worse. Bella used her influence as a bully to make every bunny in the class turn against Fluffy. She even caused Brindle to change the way she treated Fluffy! Brindle was afraid to stand up for her friend. As a result, Fluffy's heart got stung with rejection and disrespect. We are all able to influence others, negatively in a hurtful way or positively in a helpful way. We have the power to sweeten someone's heart with honey, or to bitter it with a sting.

Sharing My Life Stories with My Child

How have I grown in influencing others in positive ways?

As a child, did I have influence? How did I use it to help or hurt others?

How did others use their influence to help or hurt me?

Looking back, what have I learned about influence and how might I have done things better?

What story can I share to inspire my child?

"You can never really live anyone else's life, not even your child's. The influence you exert is through your own life, and what you've become yourself."
—ELEANOR ROOSEVELT

Putting Myself in My Child's Shoes...Influence & Bullying

How can I encourage my child to grow in influencing others in positive ways?

How do I see my child using their influence?

Is my child being bullied? Or being the bully? If not, how do they treat bullies and those being bullied?

How might I use my story to encourage my child to use their influence in positive ways?

"It's not our job to toughen up our child to face a cruel and heartless world. It's our job to raise child who will make the world a little less cruel and heartless."
—L.R. KNOST

What Could I Possibly Say to Encourage My Child?

How were you able to use positive influence with your friends?
That's such a great and wise way to behave!

Can you recall the time you used of
negative influence and why you did it?
If you let your emotions control you, it can lead
you to do things you don't mean to do.

Which one of your friends influences you the most? Why?
You are such an interesting child!

Do you remember a time when you were
influenced on a negative way?
Don't give in! You have so much to share with others!

What I will choose to say when I see that my child dealing with positive and negative influences? Or influencing others?

_____

_____

_____

*HIDE THE BUNNY!
Or ask the Parent to tell you where it is hidden,
and confirm Adventure Challenge Date with Parent!
(date) _____ (time) _____

"Parents are the ultimate role models for children. Every word, movement and action have an effect. No other person or outside force has a greater influence on a child than the parent."
—BEN KEESHAN

Adventure Challenge Date
WEEK 5: INFLUENCE & BULLYING

"I LOVE YOU, FIRST, FOREMOST AND FOREVER. NOW LET'S HAVE FUN!"

1. Have you ever had someone bully you? How did you feel? What was your reaction?
2. Jealousy happens when we feel we are not as good as others. Have you ever helped a jealous friend discover their own unique gifts so they could shine, without stopping others from shining?
3. Have you ever been the bully yourself? What caused you to choose to act that way?
4. Would you like to hear a story about influence and bullying from my own life? (Share from your journal)
5. Is there anything else you'd like to talk about?

BUNNY ON THE MOVE!

Let's find the bunny! *(Play Hot & Cold—Hide & Seek)*
What is our new word for next week? *Adventures*
Let's glue it to your poster. Wow, we're making progress!

Tracking My Trek
THE WEEK IN REVIEW

What cool things or concerns did I discover about myself this week?

What cool things or concerns did I discover about my child this week?

How did I use my life story to encourage my child?

What new thing might I try in the future because of my discoveries?

WEEK 6: ADVENTURES OF DISCOVERY

PEEKING INTO MY CHILD'S ACTIVITY BOOK...

KAI-PONO

Kai-Pono,
if you are real and true,
I need to see you
and talk to you!"
She kept tugging on her ear
and feeling so sorry for herself
that she didn't even know
she was on the wrong trail..

ADVENTURE

An adventure is an exciting experience of discovery! Fluffy tugs on her ear whenever she is afraid or feels sorry for herself. Instead of helping, it distracts her from seeing what's truly important. She didn't even know she was on the wrong trail! Fluffy did a smart thing when she called out to the wisest name she knew. Kai-Pono listened and invited Fluffy on a grand adventure of discovery! Life itself is an adventure. Some discoveries are fun and exciting. Some experiences are hard and scary...but if we are open to learn, even those can teach us important lessons and help us grow strong in noble character.

Sharing My Life Stories with My Child

How have I grown through adventures?

As a child, what were my favorite adventures?
Did I have a bad one?

How do I feel about adventures today?
Am I in the midst of one?

Looking back, what do I wish I could have experienced or done differently?

What story can I share to inspire my child?

"Not all classrooms have four walls."
—ANON

Putting Myself in My Child's Shoes...Adventures

How can I encourage my child to grow through adventures?

Has my child experienced a favorite adventure? Have they had a bad one?

What exciting adventure could I plan with my child?

How might I use my story to encourage my child to embrace new discoveries?

Are there other stories I might share?

"Kids go where there is excitement. They stay where there is love."
—ZIG ZIGLAR

What Could I Possibly Say to Encourage My Child?

Is there any adventure you'd like us to do as a family?
What is it?
If you could choose to go on any adventure with your friends,
what would that be?

What's your most thrilling memory?
Tell me your favorite memory of something
we did together and had tons of fun.

How do you feel when you are out of your comfort zone?
It's ok not to feel comfortable about something new.
Is there something you would like to try
but feel afraid? What is it?

What does "going on an adventure" means to you?
I love how curious you are about discovering new things!

What I will choose to say to my child about embracing adventures of discovery?

_____

_____

*HIDE THE BUNNY!
Or ask the Parent to tell you where it is hidden,
and confirm Adventure Challenge Date with Parent!
(date) _____ (time) _____

"Educating the mind without educating
the heart is no education at all."
—ARISTOTLE

Adventure Challenge Date
WEEK 6: ADVENTURE

"I LOVE YOU, FIRST, FOREMOST AND FOREVER. NOW LET'S HAVE FUN!"

1. What did you learn this week in your Adventure Activity Book about Adventure?
2. Have you ever felt like nobody liked you and something was wrong with you? What made you feel that way?
3. Have you ever cried out for help? How was your experience?
4. How would you feel if Kai-Pono invited you on an adventure?
5. Would you like to hear a story about adventure from my own life? (Share from your journal)
6. Is there anything else you'd like to talk about?

BUNNY ON THE MOVE!

Let's find the bunny! *(Play Hot & Cold—Hide & Seek)*
What is our new word for next week? *Empathy*
Let's glue it to your poster. Wow, we're making progress!

"Love is giving your kids your undivided attention and time."
—KEVIN HEATH

Tracking My Trek
THE WEEK IN REVIEW

What cool things or concerns did I discover about myself this week?

What cool things or concerns did I discover about my child this week?

How did I use my life story to encourage my child?

What new thing might I try in the future because of my discoveries?

WEEK 7: EMPATHY

PEEKING INTO MY CHILD'S ACTIVITY BOOK...

A NEW PERSPECTIVE

"I know every bunny by name
and my keen ears can hear
every word spoken
in the land of Lakana.
Though you did not see me,
I walked home with you
from the Wild Woods.
And I felt the stings
that made you cry this morning.'"

EMPATHY

Empathy means understanding how someone feels and showing them how much you care. Empathy is important in a healthy friendship! It helps you see how your actions can hurt or help others. It takes you out of your own world and puts you into "someone else's shoes." Kai-Pono put himself into Fluffy's shoes and felt the stings in her heart. Then he helped her look through his eyes to give her a new perspective. Have you ever felt upset when a friend got hurt? That's empathy! Have you ever noticed your mama feeling frustrated as she puts away your toys after a long day at work? If you're able to see how she might feel, that's empathy and helping her shows how much you care and love her!

Sharing My Life Stories with My Child

How have I grown in showing empathy?

As a child, was I able to understand how others felt? If so, how did I show them that I cared?

Was there anyone who came alongside me and showed empathy? How did it help me?

Looking back, what have I learned as an adult that has helped me show more empathy to those around me?

What story can I share to inspire my child?

"If there is any one secret of success, it lies in the ability to get the other person's point of view and see things from his angle as well as your own."
—HENRY FORD

Putting Myself in My Child's Shoes...Empathy

How can I encourage my child to grow in empathy toward others?

How do I see my child showing empathy towards others?

How might I show empathy toward my child?

How might I use my story to encourage my child to grow in empathy and use it wisely?

Are there other stories I might share?

"No one cares how much you know, until they know how much you care."
—THEODORE ROOSEVELT

What Could I Possibly Say to Encourage My Child?

Tell me, what's going on inside your heart?
How have you been feeling about your friends lately?

I feel how hurt you are, I'm sorry.
How can I help you?

You are doing so well in being sensitive to those around you!
I really appreciate what you've done! Thank you!

How are your friends doing?
It's very kind of you to consider how your friends feel.
I love your gentle caring heart!

What can you say when someone is hurting?
How can you show them that you care?

Do you struggle getting other's point of view?
How can I help you?

What will I choose to say to show my child how much I care and to help my child grow in empathy toward others?

_____
_____

*HIDE THE BUNNY!
Or ask the Parent to tell you where it is hidden,
and confirm Adventure Challenge Date with Parent!
(date) _____ (time) _____

Adventure Challenge Date
WEEK 7: EMPATHY

"I LOVE YOU, FIRST, FOREMOST AND FOREVER. NOW LET'S HAVE FUN!"

1. What did you learn this week in your Adventure Activity Book about Empathy?
2. Is there any adventure you were not able to enjoy because of bad thoughts at that moment? If that happens again, how might you stop those thoughts?
3. Tell me about a time when you had the opportunity to look at your own life through new eyes and gain a new perspective?
4. Is there someone who might be able to help you do that?
5. Would you like to hear a story about empathy from my own life? (Share from your journal)
6. Is there anything else you'd like to talk about?

BUNNY ON THE MOVE!

Let's find the bunny! *(Play Hot & Cold—Hide & Seek)*
What is our new word for next week? *Celebration*
Let's glue it to your poster. Wow, we're making progress!

Tracking My Trek
THE WEEK IN REVIEW

What cool things or concerns did I discover about myself this week?

What cool things or concerns did I discover about my child this week?

How did I use my life story to encourage my child?

What new thing might I try in the future because of my discoveries?

WEEK 8: CELEBRATION

PEEKING INTO MY CHILD'S ACTIVITY BOOK...

CELEBRATION

Birds sang. Squirrels chattered.
A beaver slapped his tail.
Fluffy had to shout
to make herself heard.
"Is it always so noisy up here?"
"I told them you were coming.
They're celebrating you!"
"Celebrating me?"

CELEBRATION

Kai-Pono invited the animals for a celebration to show Fluffy how special she was to him. Celebrating one another is more important than you may think! We have the power to help others feel loved. A celebration is a very special way of lifting someone up and showing them how important they are to you. And guess what! You don't have to wait for a birthday to do it!

"Family dinners are the one activity found to foster the greatest child development."
—DEBORAH NORVILLE

Sharing My Life Stories with My Child

How have I grown in celebrating others?

As a child, was there ever a time I was celebrated? What did it look like and how did I feel?

How did I ever help to celebrate someone else?

Looking back, what have I learned as an adult about the power of celebrations to help others feel loved and cherished? Or not?

What story can I share to inspire my child?

Putting Myself in My Child's Shoes...Celebrations

How can I encourage my child to grow in celebrating others?

Have I seen my child being celebrated? How did my child react?

How might I celebrate my child to show how much I love and cherish them?

How might I use my story to help my child understand the power of celebrations?

Are there other stories I might share?

"Play is often talked about as if it were a relief from serious learning. But for children, play is serious learning. Play is really the work of childhood."
—FRED ROGERS

What Could I Possibly Say to Encourage My Child?

You did so well in your exam! How would you like to celebrate it?
You are my treasure and you make me so happy!

Is there anyone you'd like to celebrate and need my help to do it?

My hugs and kisses are a way to celebrate you and
let you know how special you are to me!

When was the last time you felt celebrated? How was it?
Do you ever feel celebrated by your friends?

What makes you feel celebrated the most?
I love playing with you! Do you feel celebrated when I do it?

What I will choose to say or do to help my child feel celebrated and to help my child celebrate others?

_____
_____
_____

*HIDE THE BUNNY!
Or ask the Parent to tell you where it is hidden,
and confirm Adventure Challenge Date with Parent!
(date) _____ (time) _____

"As your kids grow, they may forget what you said,
but they won't forget how you made them feel."
—KEVIN HEATH

Adventure Challenge Date
WEEK 8: CELEBRATION

Seek first to understand, then to be understood!

"I LOVE YOU, FIRST, FOREMOST AND FOREVER NOW LET'S HAVE FUN!"

1. What did you learn in your Adventure Activity Book this week about Celebration?
2. Have you ever been celebrated? Did you feel loved?
3. What does it mean to celebrate someone?
4. Who in your life could you celebrate to help them feel loved? What might that look like?
5. Would you like to hear a story about celebration from my own life? (Share from your journal)
6. Is there anything else you'd like to talk about?

BUNNY ON THE MOVE!

Let's find the bunny! *(Play Hot & Cold—Hide & Seek)*
What is our new word for next week? *Courage*
Let's glue it to your poster. Wow, we're making progress!

Tracking My Trek
THE WEEK IN REVIEW

What cool things or concerns did I discover about myself this week?

What cool things or concerns did I discover about my child this week?

How did I use my life story to encourage my child?

What new thing might I try in the future because of my discoveries?

WEEK 9: COURAGE & CONFIDENCE

PEEKING INTO MY CHILD'S ACTIVITY BOOK...

THE ROAR

"King Kai-Pono,
why would you go to all this trouble for me?
I'm a no-bunny."
The King growled a low unhappy growl.
"The stings we give ourselves can hurt even more
than those we receive from others!"
Then his voice grew warm.
"You are special to me, Fluffy!
Who said you were a no-bunny?"
Her chin began to tremble.
"It's just how I feel."

COURAGE

Courage means saying 'YES to a good thing, even if it's scary, because it's important to do it! After Fluffy received stings of rejection from Bonzo and Bella, she stung herself with the lie that she was a "no-bunny." But Kai-Pono taught her that not everything we feel is really true! Being a smart bunny, she used courage to say YES when Kai-Pono invited her to let go of her dark lies and receive his roar that filled her with courage and confidence and even love.

"Courage is the most important of all the virtues because without courage, you can't practice any other virtue consistent."
—MAYA ANGELOU

Sharing My Life Stories with My Child

How have I grown in courage and confidence?

As a child, how did I ever use courage to do something a bit hard or scary?

What did I see others doing that demonstrated courage to me?

Looking back, what have I learned about courage and how might I handle things differently now than I did as a child?

What story can I share to inspire my child?

Putting Myself in My Child's Shoes...Courage & Confidence

How can I encourage my child to grow in courage and confidence?

How have I seen my child demonstrate courage? Or confidence?

Is there a situation they are facing now that requires courage?

How might I use my story to encourage my child to develop a courageous heart?

Are there other stories I might share?

"Don't handicap your child by making their lives easy."
—ROBERT A. HEINLEIN

What Could I Possibly Say to Encourage My Child?

You were so courageous! I'm glad you are my child!
It's ok if you don't get right the first time.
At least you were being brave enough to try!
It takes courage to tell the truth. You may not feel brave,
but you're one of the bravest people I know!
What's wrong with my warrior?
None of us were made to be perfect,
but we can defeat our fears by not giving up.

Being courageous is about taking a chance
even when you don't feel ready yet for something...
At times I don't feel I'm strong either.
But I remind myself of what's more important than my fears!

I love that you speak up for what you feel is right,
but yelling is not the best way to do it.
Yelling is not an act of courage...
(when courageous but with wrong attitude)

What I will choose to say when I see that my child is struggling with courage?

---

*HIDE THE BUNNY!
Or ask the Parent to tell you where it is hidden,
and confirm Adventure Challenge Date with Parent!
(date) _____ (time) _____

"First, think. Second, believe. Third, dream. And finally, dare."
—WALT DISNEY

Adventure Challenge Date
WEEK 9: COURAGE & CONFIDENCE

"I LOVE YOU, FIRST, FOREMOST AND FOREVER. NOW LET'S HAVE FUN!"

1. What did you learn in your Adventure Activity Book this week about Courage?
2. Who are the people in your life that have shown you love? Do those people also have courage and confidence?
3. Fluffy pulls on her ear when she thinks unhappy thoughts. What do you do?
4. How might you handle a hard situation in your life if you were full of confidence and courage and love?
5. Would you like to hear a story about courage and confidence from my own life? (Share from your journal)
6. Is there anything else you'd like to talk about?

BUNNY ON THE MOVE!

Let's find the bunny! *(Play Hot & Cold—Hide & Seek)*
What is our new word for next week? *Love*
Let's glue it to your poster. Wow, we're making progress!

Tracking My Trek
THE WEEK IN REVIEW

What cool things or concerns did I discover about myself this week?

_____
_____
_____

What cool things or concerns did I discover about my child this week?

_____
_____
_____

How did I use my life story to encourage my child?

_____
_____
_____

What new thing might I try in the future because of my discoveries?

_____
_____
_____

WEEK 10: FULL OF LOVE

PEEKING INTO MY CHILD'S ACTIVITY BOOK...

FLUFFULL

And now that your own heart is full,
you have a very important purpose
in the land of Lakana."
"I do?"
"Yes!"
Your heart of gold that's full and bright
can bring courage and love and light
to every bunny you meet!
You can help heal hurting hearts."
"It's just how I feel."

FULL OF LOVE

Full of Love means wanting the very best for others. Fluffull now wants the very best for her friends! Her new purpose is to bring love and light to hurting bunnies as they meet her soft heart. Fluffull sees that the more she reaches out to help others, the more she becomes her best-self! Instead of holding stings inside her heart and stinging others from her own hurts, she lets go of her hurts and gains confidence in the truth of who she is. Now she knows she can bring courage, love and light to her friends!

"My mom and dad gave their kids the greatest gift of all—the gift of unconditional love. They cared deeply about who we would be, and much less about what we would do."
—MITT ROMNEY

Sharing My Life Stories with My Child

How have I grown in being full of love?

As a child, how did I receive love or light in my life? Did someone want the very best for me?

How did I reach out to others to share love and light with them? And strive to promote the very best for their life?

Looking back, what do I wish were different and what have I learned about the value of love?

What story can I share to inspire my child?

Putting Myself in My Child's Shoes...Being Full of Love

How can I encourage my child to grow in being full of love?

Is my child filled with love and light? If not, how might I help them experience it?

Does my child want the very best for others? How have I seen my child reach out to others to share love and light with them?

How might I use my story to encourage my child to share love and light with the world?

Are there other stories I might share?

> "Try to see your child as a seed that came in a packet without a label. Your job is to provide the right environment and nutrients and to pull the weeds. You can't decide what kind of flower you'll get or in which season it will bloom."
> —ANONYMOUS

What Could I Possibly Say to Encourage My Child?

When you're gone, I miss you every minute!
Our family wouldn't be the same without you...
I feel so loved by you
when you share and trust your life with me.

How did you love your friends and family well this week?
What makes you feel loved the most by me?

The world is such a better place because you're in it!
I love and care for you so deeply!

Is there any sting in your heart that you would
like to share with me so you can let go of it?

What I will choose to say to my child to show that my heart is full of love and to help them love their friends well?

_____
_____
_____

*HIDE THE BUNNY!
Or ask the Parent to tell you where it is hidden,
and confirm Adventure Challenge Date with Parent!
(date) _____ (time) _____

"Love is giving your kids your undivided attention and time."
—KEVIN HEATH

Adventure Challenge Date
WEEK 10: FULL OF LOVE

"I LOVE YOU, FIRST, FOREMOST AND FOREVER. NOW LET'S HAVE FUN!"

1. What did you learn in your Adventure Activity Book this week about being Full of Love?
2. What does your name mean? Does it fit you well?
3. What do you love about your name?
4. How can you bring courage and love and light to the people around you?
5. Would you like to hear a story about being full of love from my own life? (Share from your journal)
6. Is there anything else you'd like to talk about?

BUNNY ON THE MOVE!

Let's find the bunny! *(Play Hot & Cold—Hide & Seek)*
What is our new word for next week? *Giving*
Let's glue it to your poster. Wow, we're making progress!

Tracking My Trek
THE WEEK IN REVIEW

What cool things or concerns did I discover about myself this week?

What cool things or concerns did I discover about my child this week?

How did I use my life story to encourage my child?

What new thing might I try in the future because of my discoveries?

WEEK 11: GIVING

PEEKING INTO MY CHILD'S ACTIVITY BOOK...

THE FLUFFULL TREE

"I made it just for you!
Whenever you feel sad, remember your tree.
Fluffull, will you ride on my back
and be my friend?"
Fluffull was so surprised she could barely speak.
"You want me to be your friend?"
Her heart felt like a balloon about to burst.
"I would be so honored to be your friend!
I love riding on your back!
You're the best friend in the whole wide world!"

GIVING

Kai-Pono showed Fluffull how special and unique she is to him by GIVING her the gifts of a new name and a tree. He also gave her a new purpose! After she let go of the bitter stings in her heart, she was able to find the good in her friends and to love them well. She couldn't care about their hearts while she was busy thinking about her own stings. Now she has the power to give the best gift a friend can ever give, the gift that Kai-Pono had given to her: True Friendship!

*"A kind gesture can reach a wound that
only compassion can heal."*
—STEVEN MARABOLI

Sharing My Life Stories with My Child

How have I grown in being more generous and giving?

As a child, how did I ever receive a special gift? How did I feel?

Did I ever make a special gift for someone? What was it and how did they react?

Looking back, what have I learned about the importance of having a generous giving heart?

What story can I share to inspire my child?

Putting Myself in My Child's Shoes...Giving

How can I encourage my child to grow in being more generous and giving?

Has my child ever received a special tailor-made give just for them? What gift might I give?

Have I ever seen my child make a special gift for someone? Or could I help them make one?

How might I use my story to encourage my child to develop a generous giving heart?

Are there other stories I might share?

"Do your little bit of good where you are; it's those little bits of good put together that overwhelm the world."
—DESMOND TUTU

What Could I Possibly Say to Encourage My Child?

Would you like to learn how to live out the spirit of giving?
Volunteer to help someone by giving your time to them.
Ask in what ways they need your help.
I'll give you a three-part piggy bank—
one section for saving, one for spending, and one for giving.
You get to choose which charity we will give to today.
How does it make you feel when you make
a difference in someone's life?
I'd love to have you with me at this community project!
I'm so proud for you taking the time to
help me! It's so kind of you!
Would you like me to fix us some hot
chocolate with marshmallows?
You have such a generous heart!
Sweet one, is giving a struggle to you? Why?
May I help you?

What I will choose to say to my child about the joy of giving?

___

*HIDE THE BUNNY!
Or ask the Parent to tell you where it is hidden,
and confirm Adventure Challenge Date with Parent!
(date) _____ (time) _____

"When you are kind to others, it not only
changes you, it changes the world."
—HAROLD KUSHNER

Adventure Challenge Date
WEEK 11: GIVING

"I LOVE YOU, FIRST, FOREMOST AND FOREVER. NOW LET'S HAVE FUN!"

1. What did you learn in your Adventure Activity Book this week about Giving?
2. Have you ever made something special for someone? If so, what was it? How did you feel about giving such a special gift?
3. Has anyone ever made anything special just for you? If so, what was it and how did you feel?
4. If Kai-Pono made something special just for you, what would you wish it would be?
5. Would you like to hear a story about giving from my own life? (Share from your journal)
6. Is there anything else you'd like to talk about?

BUNNY ON THE MOVE!

Let's find the bunny! *(Play Hot & Cold—Hide & Seek)*
What is our new word for next week? *Patience*
Let's glue it to your poster. Wow, we're making progress!

Tracking My Trek
THE WEEK IN REVIEW

What cool things or concerns did I discover about myself this week?

What cool things or concerns did I discover about my child this week?

How did I use my life story to encourage my child?

What new thing might I try in the future because of my discoveries?

WEEK 12: PATIENCE

PEEKING INTO MY CHILD'S ACTIVITY BOOK...

DIAMONDS IN THE ROUGH

"But they are not kind," she whined.
I wonder why they were born!"
"I have told you enough
to love your friends well.
But you must choose
to find the good in them.
I'm asking you, Fluffull
To be patient with your friends,
and with yourself!"

PATIENCE

Patience means waiting for the good thing you want, without getting angry or upset. Fluffull wants her friends to like her. She now knows it's important to be PATIENT and kind as they grow, even when they are not kind to her. She sees that every bunny in her life was born for a reason. Just like her, they have stories to tell that explain why they are the way they are. She now has the power to choose to love them well while she waits for them to grow.

"Stop trying to perfect your child, but keep trying to perfect your relationship with him."
—DR. HENKER

Sharing My Life Stories with My Child

How have I grown in patience?

As a child, was I able to patient with my friends and stay calm even when things went wrong?

As an adult, how have I learned to be patient with myself and my family?

Looking back, would I have done anything different if I looked for the GOOD in everyone?

What story can I share to inspire my child?

Putting Myself in My Child's Shoes...Being Patient

How can I encourage my child to grow in patience?

How have I demonstrated patience with my child?

How have I ever seen my child demonstrate patience?

How might I use my story to encourage my child to develop patience with family and friends?

Are there other stories I might share?

> "Tantrums are not bad behavior. Tantrums are an expression of emotion that became too much for the child to bear. No punishment is required. What your child needs is compassion and safe, loving arms to unload in."
> —REBECCA EANES

What Could I Possibly Say to Encourage My Child?

It brings me joy to see you waiting for your turn to speak!
Look how much you are growing in patience!

I know it's no fun to wait in line,
but waiting patiently shows respect to those around you.
When is it hardest for you to be patient?

How have you been patient with your friends this week?
Being patient is like waiting nicely without whining.

Would you like to put a puzzle together with me?
It can help us grow in patience while we we have fun together!

Being patient with your siblings
shows how much you care about them.
Breathe deeply and remember your happiest moments!

What I will choose to say when I see my child struggling to be patient?

_____

_____

*HIDE THE BUNNY!
Or ask the Parent to tell you where it is hidden,
and confirm Adventure Challenge Date with Parent!
(date) _____ (time) _____

> "Don't limit a child to your own learning,
> for he was born in another time."
> —RABINDRANATH TAGORE

Adventure Challenge Date
WEEK 12: BEING PATIENT & POSITIVE

"I LOVE YOU, FIRST, FOREMOST AND FOREVER. NOW LET'S HAVE FUN!"

1. What did you learn in your Adventure Activity Book this week about being Patient and Positive?
2. What negative thoughts have you had about your friends because you didn't understand why they are the way they are? How can you be patient while they grow?
3. Have you ever wondered why you are the way you are, both in looks and personality? What gifts can you share? Can you be patient with yourself as you grow?
4. Have you ever wondered why your friends are the way they are? Can you list the positive things you see in them while waiting for them to grow?
5. Would you like to hear a story about that patience my own life? (Share from your journal)
6. Is there anything else you'd like to talk about?

BUNNY ON THE MOVE!

Let's find the bunny! *(Play Hot & Cold—Hide & Seek)* What is our new word for next week? *Perseverence* Let's glue it to your poster. Wow, we're making progress!

104

Tracking My Trek
THE WEEK IN REVIEW

What cool things or concerns did I discover about myself this week?

What cool things or concerns did I discover about my child this week?

How did I use my life story to encourage my child?

What new thing might I try in the future because of my discoveries?

WEEK 13: PERSEVERENCE

PEEKING INTO MY CHILD'S ACTIVITY BOOK...

STORM CLOUDS

"Where is he taking me?
She reached up to tug on her ear.
And that's how she lost her grip on his mane
and slid right off his back.
THUNK!!
The next thing she knew,
she was lying in a puddle of black muddy goo.
She was so busy looking at the yucky stuff on her fur
that she didn't see Kai-Pono
waiting patiently on the path ahead of her."

PERSEVERENCE

Perseverance means grabbing onto your goal and not letting go, even when it's hard or scary. Fluffull let go of her goal of staying with Kai-Pono on their great adventure! That's when she fell and things got really scary! It's easy to get distracted by things that takes our eyes away from our goal. It's important to us, and those around us, that we persevere in reaching our goal... on our Trek to the Summit! Our noble character will make a huge difference in our lives.

"Where parents do too much for their child, the child will not do much for themselves."
—ELBERT HUBBARD

Sharing My Life Stories with My Child

How can I grow in perseverance?

As a child, was there a situation when I needed to persevere in spite of obstacles?

How have I learned to persevere as an adult?

Looking back, would anything be different if I had persevered?

What story can I share to inspire my child?

Putting Myself in My Child's Shoes...Perseverence

How can I encourage my child to grow in perseverance?

How have I ever persevered with my child?

How have I seen my child persevere?

How might I use my story to encourage my child to develop perseverance when frustrated?

Are there other stories I might share?

"But kids don't stay with you if you do it right. It's the one job where, the better you are, the more surely you won't be needed in the long run."
—BARBARA KINGSOLVER

What Could I Possibly Say to Encourage My Child?

*I admire the way you keep trying without giving up.
It's ok if you didn't get it right this time...
failing is part of how we learn, it makes us stronger.
What has challenged you lately?
How have you struggled with it?
It may be hard, but you can do it! I believe in you!
You have so much potential!
Once you overcome the first hard step,
the second won't seem as hard.
I'm here for you if you need me!
All the most important goals take time
and dedication to come true.
I understand you may be frustrated that it's hard,
but I'm here for you!*

What I will choose to say when I see that my child is struggling to persevere?

_____
_____
_____

*HIDE THE BUNNY!
Or ask the Parent to tell you where it is hidden,
and confirm Adventure Challenge Date with Parent!

(date) _____ (time) _____

"Never help a child with a task at which he feels he can succeed."
—MARIA MONTESSORI

Adventure Challenge Date
WEEK 13: PERSEVERENCE

"I LOVE YOU, FIRST, FOREMOST AND FOREVER. NOW LET'S HAVE FUN!"

1. What did you learn this week in your Adventure Activity Book about Perseverance?
2. Have you ever had a very pleasant experience, only to have a "storm" hit afterward, stealing all the joy you felt? What happened? What did you do while the storm raged on?
3. How do you react when you're suddenly afraid?
4. How might you remember the good things you know to be true when things start to go bad?
5. Would you like to hear a story perseverance that from my own life? (Share from your journal)
6. Is there anything else you'd like to talk about?

BUNNY ON THE MOVE!

Let's find the bunny! *(Play Hot & Cold—Hide & Seek)*
What is our new word for next week? *Fear*
Let's glue it to your poster. Wow, we're making progress!

Tracking My Trek
THE WEEK IN REVIEW

What cool things or concerns did I discover about myself this week?

What cool things or concerns did I discover about my child this week?

How did I use my life story to encourage my child?

What new thing might I try in the future because of my discoveries?

WEEK 14: FEAR

PEEKING INTO MY CHILD'S ACTIVITY BOOK...

COYOTES

Fluffull was no dumb bunny. She knew those coyotes would eat her for supper! She looked frantically for a place to hide...

FEAR

Fear is the feeling that warns you when something dangerous or harmful is about to happen, so you can seek safety. "Smart fear" is very important because it warns you of true danger and makes you take actions that could save your life. "Dumb fear" tells you you're not good enough to try something and holds you back from becoming your best self. "Dumb fear" must be faced with courage. It's important that we listen to our fears long enough to discover if they are "smart" or "dumb" fears. Then we can decide what's the best thing to do.

"When I look back on all these worries, I remember the story of the old man who said on his deathbed that he had had a lot of trouble in his life, most of which had never happened."
—WINSTON CHURCHILL

Sharing My Life Stories with My Child

How can I grow in overcoming fear?

As a child, when did I feel "smart fear" that helped me identify true danger and seek safety?

When did I feel "dumb fear" that kept me from trying a new experience?

Looking back, how might things have gone differently if I had paid more attention to my fears?

What story can I share to inspire my child?

Putting Myself in My Child's Shoes...Fear

How can I encourage my child to grow in overcoming fear?

When have I seen my child experience "smart fear" to avoid real danger?

When have I seen my child allow "dumb fear" to hold them back from a new experience?

How might I use my story to help my child identify "smart" and "dumb" fears?

Are there other stories I might share?

"Expose yourself to your deepest fear; after that, fear has no power, and the fear of freedom shrinks and vanishes. You are free."
—JIM MORRISON

What Could I Possibly Say to Encourage My Child?

*I understand how you feel.
You don't need to face your fear alone, I'm here for you!
Your fears are important to me!*

Wow that sounds really scary! I've been scared as a child too. What can make you feel safer?

What do you think is causing you to be afraid of that?

Remember when you were afraid of _____ at first and then you really had fun?

Would you like to take a walk to calm your worried mind? Let's talk to your fears and tell them all the positives about this situation.

Let me tell you what I know about handling fear.

What I will choose to say when I see that my child is struggling with fear?

_____

_____

*HIDE THE BUNNY!
Or ask the Parent to tell you where it is hidden, and confirm Adventure Challenge Date with Parent!

(date) _____ (time) _____

"Fear makes the wolf bigger than he is."
—GERMAN PROVERB

Adventure Challenge Date
WEEK 14: FEAR

"I LOVE YOU, FIRST, FOREMOST AND FOREVER, NOW LET'S HAVE FUN!"

1. What did you learn in your Adventure Activity Book this week about Fear?
2. Have you ever been in a situation where something or somebody wanted to hurt you? What happened? Who did you call out to for help?
3. How have smart fears protected you from real danger?
4. How have dumb fears kept you from trying something new?
5. Would you like to hear a story about fear from my own life? (Share from your journal)
6. Is there anything else you'd like to talk about?

BUNNY ON THE MOVE!

Let's find the bunny! *(Play Hot & Cold—Hide & Seek)*
What is our new word for next week? *Honesty*
Let's glue it to your poster. Wow, we're making progress!

Tracking My Trek
THE WEEK IN REVIEW

What cool things or concerns did I discover about myself this week?

What cool things or concerns did I discover about my child this week?

How did I use my life story to encourage my child?

What new thing might I try in the future because of my discoveries?

WEEK 15: HONESTY

PEEKING INTO MY CHILD'S ACTIVITY BOOK...

ONI

Fluffull asked, "What is your name?"
"It was Veronica.
But the King changed it to Oni
because I'm honest
and I always tell the truth."
"I'm Fluff... Fluffull!
And I'm so glad I stumbled into you today."

HONESTY

Honesty is choosing to tell the truth and act with honor. It is one of the most important noble qualities a person can have. Being honest and trustworthy go hand in hand. Your honesty gives you the courage to remain honorable. Being trustworthy means others can respect you and trust you to be true to your word.

"Integrity is doing the right thing, even when no one is watching."
—C.S. LEWIS

Sharing My Life Stories with My Child

How can I grow in honesty?

As a child, was there an experience that taught me about the importance of being honest?

How important was it to me that my family and friends were honest with me?

Looking back, how might things have been gone differently if honesty had been used?

What story can I share to inspire my child?

Putting Myself in My Child's Shoes...Honesty

How can I encourage my child to grow in honesty?

How have I seen my child demonstrate honesty?

How have I demonstrated honesty with my child?

How might I use my story to help my child see the importance of being honest with family and friends?

Are there other stories I might share?

"Honesty is more than not lying. It is truth telling, truth speaking, truth living, and truth loving."
—JAMES E. FAUST

What Could I Possibly Say to Encourage My Child?

What do you think it means to be honest?
When was the last time you were not honest?
How did it affect others? And yourself?

How would you feel if I lied to you?
Would it make you trust me more or less?

Truth is better than lying or hiding something.
That way we can find solutions that really work!
Not being truthful can only hurt others.

Thank you for your honesty! I admire you so much!
Honesty is the best policy.
Which friend do you believe is the most truthful? Why?
I'm so proud of you for telling me the truth!

This is not like you; you're usually honest with me.
Are you telling me the truth?

What I will choose to say when I see that my child is struggling with their honesty?

_____
_____

*HIDE THE BUNNY!
Or ask the Parent to tell you where it is hidden, and confirm Adventure Challenge Date with Parent!
(date) _____ (time) _____

"Stop trying to perfect your child, but keep trying to perfect your relationship with him."
—DR. HENKER

Adventure Challenge Date
WEEK 15: HONESTY

"I LOVE YOU, FIRST, FOREMOST AND FOREVER. NOW LET'S HAVE FUN!"

1. What did you learn in your Adventure Activity Book this week about Honesty?
2. What was the hardest time you ever had and what did you do when that happened?
3. Have you ever met someone who always tells the truth? Do you trust that person?
4. How important is it to you that people are honest?
5. Would you like to hear a story about honesty from my own life? (Share from your journal)
6. Is there anything else you'd like to talk about?

BUNNY ON THE MOVE!

Let's find the bunny! *(Play Hot & Cold—Hide & Seek)*
What is our new word for next week? *Cherish*
Let's glue it to your poster. Wow, we're making progress!

Tracking My Trek
THE WEEK IN REVIEW

What cool things or concerns did I discover about myself this week?

What cool things or concerns did I discover about my child this week?

How did I use my life story to encourage my child?

What new thing might I try in the future because of my discoveries?

WEEK 16: CHERISH

PEEKING INTO MY CHILD'S ACTIVITY BOOK...

THE RAINBOW'S END

She leaped to her feet
and dashed down the path
to find the gold
at the rainbow's end.

Sure enough,
there sat the king with his golden fur
and shimmering crown.

CHERISH

To cherish someone means to think of them as being very precious, like gold! Fluffull learned to cherish Kai-Pono, because his friendship was as precious to her as gold itself! People cherish gold because it looks pretty and was used like money to buy things. But a true friend with noble character is more precious than gold! They help us in good times and in bad times. Have you learned how to cherish your friends? And to treat them as if they are super precious to you?

> "The best inheritance a parent can give his child
> is a few minutes of his time each day."
> —ORLANDO ALOYSIUS BATTISTA

Sharing My Life Stories with My Child

How can I grow in cherishing others?

As a child, was there a person in my life who made me feel cherished?

How did I ever make someone else feel cherished?

Looking back, how might things have gone differently if I had known how to cherish a friend?

What story can I share to inspire my child?

Putting Myself in My Child's Shoes...Cherishing Others

How can I encourage my child to grow in cherishing others?

How have I seen my child cherish an animal or friend or family member?

How have I shown my child that I cherish them?

How might I use my story to help my child learn to cherish their family and friends?

Are there other stories I might share?

> "Loving a child doesn't mean giving in to all his whims; to love him is to bring out the best in him, to teach him to love what is difficult."
> —NADIA BOULANGER

What Could I Possibly Say to Encourage My Child?

*Cherishing makes the world a richer place.
Have you ever set time aside to cherish something?
Look at that astonishing sunset!*

*It's amazing to watch you cherish your animals.
I see such tenderness in your heart!*

*I love this painting you gave me. I'll cherish it always!
What memories do you cherish that fill your heart?*

*Would you like to visit someone you cherish? Who?
Could I help me to make something for a
friend so they can feel cherished?*

What I will choose to say to help my child feel cherished...
And to help my child cherish others...

_____

_____

_____

*HIDE THE BUNNY!
Or ask the Parent to tell you where it is hidden,
and confirm Adventure Challenge Date with Parent!
(date) _____ (time) _____

"Praise your child openly, reprehend them secretly."
—W. CECIL

Adventure Challenge Date
WEEK 16: CHERISH

"I LOVE YOU, FIRST, FOREMOST AND FOREVER, NOW LET'S HAVE FUN!"

1. What did you learn in your Adventure Activity Book this week about Cherishing?
2. Love never ends...the more we share, the more we have! Have you ever struggled sharing a friend that you cherish? Why was it hard and what did you do about your feelings?
3. How would you feel if you found Kai-Pono waiting for you?
4. Have you ever wondered what would be the most cherished treasure you could find at the end of the rainbow?
5. Would you like to hear a story about cherishing from my own life? (Share from your journal)
6. Is there anything else you'd like to talk about?

BUNNY ON THE MOVE!

Let's find the bunny! *(Play Hot & Cold—Hide & Seek)*
What is our new word for next week? *Encourage*
Let's glue it to your poster. Wow, we're making progress!

Tracking My Trek
THE WEEK IN REVIEW

What cool things or concerns did I discover about myself this week?

_____
_____
_____

What cool things or concerns did I discover about my child this week?

_____
_____
_____

How did I use my life story to encourage my child?

_____
_____
_____

What new thing might I try in the future because of my discoveries?

_____
_____
_____

WEEK 17: ENCOURAGE

PEEKING INTO MY CHILD'S ACTIVITY BOOK...

A TRULY GREAT FRIEND

"Remember Fluffull, that confidence means
not listening to your fear and tugging on your ear.
Hold onto to your courage tighter than ever.
We'll ride out the storms together.
Listen for my whisper
in your ear going up
and whatever you do,
don't tug on your ear going down.
That just makes you frown!"

ENCOURAGE

To encourage someone means using words that inspire courage and confidence and hope, like Kai-Pono did with Fluffull. He taught her to embrace life with courage instead of feeling sorry for herself. It's important that we encourage each other when life gets hard. Hold on to the lessons you learned and you'll be able to ride out the storms, facing every challenge that may come your way!

*"The way you see people is the way you treat them,
and the way you treat them is what they become."*
—GOETHE

Sharing My Life Stories with My Child

How can I grow in encouraging others?

As a child, who encouraged me to keep going when things became difficult?

When did I encourage someone to keep going when they wanted to give up?

Looking back, how might things have gone differently if I had or had not been encouraged?

What story can I share to inspire my child?

Putting Myself in My Child's Shoes...Encouraging Others

How can I encourage my child to grow in encouraging others?

How have I seen my child encourage someone?

How have I ever encouraged my child?

How might I use my story to help my child learn to encourage others?

Are there other stories I might share?

> ""Encourage don't belittle, embrace their individuality. And show them that no matter what, they will always have value if they stay true to themselves."
> —SOLANGE NICOLE

What Could I Possibly Say to Encourage My Child?

Why are you so glum, chum? How I help you?
Failing means you're halfway to success!
Never allow the things you cannot do
to stop you from doing what you can do!

Remember when you thought you could not do _____
and you ended up achieving it?
I know it is not easy, but patience will help
you to persevere.
I like the solution you came up with, congratulations!
I can see that you worked very hard on this.
Whatever the outcome, you are a fighter!
What makes you feel encouraged?

What I will choose to say to help my child learn to encourage others?

_____

_____

*HIDE THE BUNNY!
Or ask the Parent to tell you where it is hidden, and confirm Adventure Challenge Date with Parent!
(date) _____ (time) _____

"It is the sunlight of parental love and encouragement that enables a child to grow in competence and slowly gain mastery over his environment."
—FELCITY BAUER

Adventure Challenge Date
WEEK 17: ENCOURAGE

"I LOVE YOU, FIRST, FOREMOST AND FOREVER. NOW LET'S HAVE FUN!"

1. What did you learn in your Adventure Activity Book this week about Encouraging others?
2. Who can you trust to ride out the storms with you?
3. Have you ever noticed yourself listening more with your "down-ear" than your "up-ear"?
4. If you could have a forever friend whispering into your "up-ear" would you like that? Who is the person that encourages you the most?
5. Would you like to hear a story about encouraging others from my own life? (Share from your journal)
6. Is there anything else you'd like to talk about?

BUNNY ON THE MOVE!

Let's find the bunny! *(Play Hot & Cold—Hide & Seek)*
What is our new word for next week? *Leadership*
Let's glue it to your poster. Wow, we're almost there!

Tracking My Trek
THE WEEK IN REVIEW

What cool things or concerns did I discover about myself this week?

What cool things or concerns did I discover about my child this week?

How did I use my life story to encourage my child?

What new thing might I try in the future because of my discoveries?

WEEK 18: LEADERSHIP

PEEKING INTO MY CHILD'S ACTIVITY BOOK...

BACK TO SCHOOL

And then to Fluffull's surprise,
Bella hopped to her side.

"I've been pretty mean.
Would you forgive me?"

Fluffull smiled.
"Of course! I'm so happy you decided to come!
Maybe you can lead us back to school?"
Bella grinned. "I love to lead!"

LEADERSHIP

Leadership is having a great idea, then inviting others to join you. Bella's big idea was to turn the class against Fluffy and she bullied the class into following her. Bella will discover that admitting her mistake is super important in becoming a good leader. That's how you build trust. If the class cannot respect her, they will stop following. Fluffull's great idea was to share yummy strawberries with her class. She used courage to kindly lead her class to enjoy happy things together! Life was sweeter when they followed her. Then she encouraged Bella to resume her leadership in a positive way.

"Children must be taught how to think, not what to think."
—MARGARET MEAD

Sharing My Life Stories with My Child

How can I encourage my child to grow in leadership?

As a child, was I a leader or a follower? When was the first time I saw someone lead well?

What have I learned as an adult about leadership, good and bad?

Looking back, how might things be different if I were a good leader or if I were following a good leader as a supportive follower?

What story can I share to inspire my child?

Putting Myself in My Child's Shoes...Leadership

How have I witnessed my child to grow in leadership?

How have I seen my child lead well? Or choose who they would follow?

Which kind of a leader am I to my child?

How might I use my story to encourage my child to lead well or choose a wise leader?

Are there other stories I might share?

> ""When I approach a child, he inspires in me two sentiments—tenderness for what he is and respect for what he may become."
> —LOUIS PASTEUR

What Could I Possibly Say to Encourage My Child?

How do you feel about working in a team?
Do you feel comfortable helping others
figure out their special part on the team?
Congratulations on working together with your friends!
You're setting a great example for them.
Would you help me to lead your siblings in
housekeeping this week?
Sweetie, it is awesome that you are guiding
others in the right path!
Would you take the lead in caring for our pet?
It's so noble of you to think about the wellbeing of your friends!
I'm proud that you're growing in being a leader!

What I will choose to say to inspire my child to grow as a leader...Or as a strong follower...?

_____
_____

*HIDE THE BUNNY!
Or ask the Parent to tell you where it is hidden,
and confirm Adventure Challenge Date with Parent!
(date) _____ (time) _____

"Children are the living messages we
send to a time we will not see."
—JOHN F. KENNEDY

Adventure Challenge Date
WEEK 18: LEADERSHIP

"I LOVE YOU, FIRST, FOREMOST AND FOREVER. NOW LET'S HAVE FUN!"

1. What did you learn this week in your Adventure Activity Book about Leadership?
2. Have you ever been bullied into following a bad leader? Or had fun following a good leader?
3. Were you ever able to bring joy to others by leading them to do happy things together?
4. Have you ever befriended a bully and encouraged them to lead well?
5. Would you like to hear a story about leadership from my own life? (Share from your journal)
6. Is there anything else you'd like to talk about?

> **BUNNY ON THE MOVE!**
> Hurray, we've reached the Summit!

Tracking My Trek
THE WEEK IN REVIEW

What cool things or concerns did I discover about myself this week?

What cool things or concerns did I discover about my child this week?

How did I use my life story to encourage my child?

What new thing might I try in the future because of my discoveries?

SUMMIT CELEBRATION SUGGESTIONS

We hope you experienced the thrill of accomplishing a huge goal, one step at a time! How is the view? Can you see the beauty and wonder in your unique child? Did your team become truly great friends of noble character?

IT'S TIME TO CELEBRATE!
What will your celebration look like?

Date: _____

Time: _____

Place: _____

People: _____

Food: _____

Activities: _____

Stories: _____

CELEBRATION MEMORIES

YEARLY MILESTONES

Yearly Milestones Explained

A wise teacher-trainer once said, "Catch them being good!" It motivated her class to do great things.

SUGGESTIONS:
- Keep your ears open for stories about your child's noble character in action.
- Observe your child at family events.
- Listen for stories from the parents.
- Watch for your child in newspaper articles.
- Then record it in your journal!
- Or jot an entry each year on their birthday…and call to tell them what you wrote!
- Present the journal to them as a gift on their grade-school graduation.

THESE PAGES WILL BE CHERISHED TREASURES IN THE YEARS TO COME!

Watching My Child Grow Through the Years...

Year _____ Age _____

How my child has demonstrated their noble character in awesome ways!

Watching My Child Grow Through the Years...

Year _____ Age _____

How my child has demonstrated their noble character in awesome ways!

_____
_____
_____
_____
_____
_____
_____
_____
_____
_____
_____
_____
_____
_____
_____
_____

Watching My Child Grow Through the Years...

Year _____ Age _____

How my child has demonstrated their noble character in awesome ways!

Watching My Child Grow Through the Years...

Year _____ Age _____

How my child has demonstrated their noble character in awesome ways!

_____
_____
_____
_____
_____
_____
_____
_____
_____
_____
_____
_____
_____
_____
_____
_____
_____

Watching My Child Grow Through the Years...

Year _____   Age _____

How my child has demonstrated their noble character in awesome ways!

Watching My Child Grow Through the Years...

Year _____ Age _____

How my child has demonstrated their noble character in awesome ways!

_____
_____
_____
_____
_____
_____
_____
_____
_____
_____
_____
_____
_____
_____
_____
_____
_____
_____
_____

Watching My Child Grow Through the Years...

Year _____ Age _____

How my child has demonstrated their noble character in awesome ways!

_____
_____
_____
_____
_____
_____
_____
_____
_____
_____
_____
_____
_____
_____
_____
_____
_____

CPSIA information can be obtained
at www.ICGtesting.com
Printed in the USA
BVHW062333210819
556456BV00001B/1/P